Psalm 23

& Jesus' Two Great Commandments

RABBI RAMI
GUIDE TO

Psalm 23

& Jesus' Two Great Commandments

- - - Roadside Assistance for the Spiritual Traveler - - -

Spirituality
&Health
BOOKS

Rabbi Rami Guide to Psalm 23
& Jesus' Two Great Commandments:
Roadside Assistance for the Spiritual Traveler
By Rami Shapiro

© 2011 Rami Shapiro

Spirituality
&Health
BOOKS

425 Boardman Street, Suite C
Traverse City, MI 49684
www.spiritualityhealth.com

Printed in Canada.

Cover and interior design by Sandra Salamony

Cataloging-in-Publication data for this book is available
upon request.

978-0-9837270-5-7
10 9 8 7 6 5 4 3 2 1

CONTENTS

SOME TEXTS ARE MERELY TEXTS—words on a page conveying information about the past; others become touchstones—a living teaching that shapes your life in the present. As a rabbi and professor of religion, I am lucky enough to teach both types of material, texts and touchstones, and while I find value in texts, it is touchstones that I truly treasure.

In this short *Rabbi Rami Guide,* we will explore two such touchstones from the Bible, the 23rd Psalm and the Two Great Commandments of Jesus. I chose these two texts because they are touchstones for millions. The 23rd Psalm brings comfort to people in times of terrible tragedy and grief, and the Two Great Commandments of Jesus bring direction to people in times of terrible confusion and doubt.

As with all the volumes in the Rabbi Rami Guide series, this book is not a book about any religion in particular. While the 23rd Psalm and the Two Great Commandments are found in the Hebrew Bible, this is not a book about the Bible or Judaism. Nor is it a book about Christianity. It is a book about two touchstone texts that can help you in times of crises. While it is true that in order to understand these texts you must understand the deeper meanings of their words, and to do this I must explore their Jewish context and Hebrew nuances, my concern isn't with the official theologies of any faith, but with the needs of people struggling for spiritual moorings.

It is my hope that you will find touchstones for your own lives in my explorations of these two texts; that you will return to these texts and my commentaries again and again whenever you need solace and support; and that with the help of this brief *Guide*, you will deepen your own spiritual walk so that you can become a shoulder for others to lean on when they need solace and support, as well.

I wish to thank Aaron Shapiro for his help with editing the earlier drafts of this manuscript, and Victoria Sutherland for polishing the final version. I am also grateful to Matt Sutherland and the entire Spirituality & Health family for making this and the other Rabbi Rami Guides possible.

The 23rd Psalm

THE ONE HUNDRED AND FIFTY poems of *Sefer Tellihim*, the Book of Psalms, provide much of the poetry of our religious and spiritual lives. Yet one psalm above all the others calls to us most powerfully: Psalm 23, "The Lord is my shepherd." This is the psalm that comforts us when we grieve, that offers us refuge when we are lost, and that proffers hope when we are hopeless. But why? What is it about the 23rd Psalm that makes this the hymn of solace? Let me suggest four things.

First, the psalm is compact and easily memorized: only fifty-seven words in the original Hebrew, and rarely more than twice that in its various English translations. Second, it speaks to us where we are, reminding us of what is available to us now in the midst of our fear, grief, and sadness. This is not a hymn to past glory or future redemption, but an invitation to walk with God here and now. Third, Psalm 23 speaks not only *about* God, but also *to* God; shifting mid-hymn from third person to second person, from "he" to "Thou," from God as idea to God as presence. And fourth, Psalm 23 asks nothing of us, but speaks instead of the unconditional grace and gifting of God's love. We don't earn God's love; we awaken to it: God is my shepherd no matter how wayward a sheep I may be.

Psalm 23 speaks to us without artifice or abstraction, but not without metaphor. It is the task of this guide to unpack the metaphors and lay bare their meaning. In keeping with the brevity of Psalm 23, I too will be brief. But do not mistake brevity for shallowness. This guide is to be read and reread. It was not written for your bookshelf, but for your nightstand, purse, and briefcase. This book, like the psalm it explores, is meant to travel with you as you walk through the shadowed valley of your own mortality, for it is only in the immediacy of your own life that the 23rd Psalm reveals the reality of God shepherding you at every turn.

The 23rd Psalm
A Psalm of David

23:1 *The Lord is my shepherd;*
I shall not want.

23:2 *He maketh me to lie down in green pastures*
He leadeth me beside the still waters.

23:3 *He restoreth my soul:*
He leadeth me in the paths of righteousness
for His names sake.

23:4 *Yea, though I walk through the valley*
of the shadow of death,
I will fear no evil for Thou art with me;
Thy rod and Thy staff, they comfort me.

23:5 *Thou preparest a table before me in the*
presence of mine enemies,
Thou anointest my head with oil;
my cup runneth over.

23:6 *Surely goodness and mercy shall follow me*
all the days of my life, and I will dwell
*in the House of the Lord for ever.** *

---

* I have chosen to use the King James Version of the 23rd Psalm because it is the most commonly used translation among those who find the psalm both moving and healing.

A Psalm of David

THE 23RD PSALM is ascribed to David, the once and future king of the Jews. David was the youngest of eight children, a child of the tribe of Judah, and a direct descendent of Ruth the Moabite. He was a shepherd, a musician, a poet, a giant slayer, a warrior, a rebel, a king, and even a murderer. But above all, he was a lover of God.

Lovers of God seek to embrace and be embraced by the Divine, to rise above weaknesses, despite continually succumbing to them. Lovers of God may be saints, but most often they are sinners. They may be whole, but most often they are broken. They may be pure, but most often they are sullied. They may be perfect, but most often they are damaged. We have little need for saints: whole, spotless, and perfect. They can't speak to us because they do not know what it is to be us. They call us to be like them, when we are condemned to be only who we are: flawed and foolish stumblers on the way, who dare to hope that sin isn't the measure by which we are gauged, but rather another opportunity to rise up and move forward.

David speaks to us not because he was a saint, but because he was a repentant sinner. David knew what it was to succumb to evil, and he knew what it was to "turn from evil and do good" (Psalm 34:14). David doesn't judge us, because he is us. And because he is us, his poetry speaks to us.

The 23rd Psalm is a Psalm of David not simply in the sense that David may have written it, but in the sense that it speaks to us in the midst of our struggles. It is a Psalm of David in that it is the hymn of a sinner repenting of sin, and realizing that no matter how far he has fallen, God is there.

A Psalm of David

23:1 ***The Lord is my shepherd;***

I shall not want.

DESPITE THE WORK OF countless translators, the Hebrew *Adonai* (Lord) never appears in our psalm. David doesn't speak of Adonai but of YHVH, the

Ineffable Reality beyond all words and ideologies. Adonai is a patriarchal euphemism that comes into use long after David wrote this psalm. Where the noun "Lord" implies masculinity, hierarchy, fixity, power, and even militarism, the verb YHVH speaks of mystery, unconditionality, and ongoing creative liberation. It is YHVH not Adonai who is your shepherd, one unlike any other.

Human shepherds keep their flocks safe by herding them along well-worn paths. But the Divine Shepherd is not about safety. The Divine Shepherd is about freedom, justice, and compassion. Where human shepherds call their flocks back to the familiar path, God calls us to the opposite.

When God called Abram and Sarai (soon to be renamed Abraham and Sarah), God called them to leave everything they knew and to travel to an unknown land (Genesis 12:1). When God called to Moses from the Burning Bush (Exodus 3:1), God called him to leave the path he was traveling and return to Egypt to liberate the Hebrew people. Human shepherds call their flocks to return to the known; the Divine Shepherd calls us to the unknown. Human shepherds call their flocks to return to the herd; the

Divine Shepherd calls us to free us.

Abraham and Sarah are called to be a blessing to the world (Genesis 12:2); Moses is called to be a liberator (Exodus 3:10). The two are not different. The ultimate blessing is the blessing of freedom, the blessing of liberation from Mitzrayim (Egypt), literally "the narrow places" of life, the places of egotism and hubris, the places of arrogance and ignorance. It is this blessing-through-liberation that David is referencing when he says, "The Lord is my shepherd." When you recite this psalm, you realize that God is your shepherd as well; that you, no less than Abraham, Sarah, Moses, and David, are called to be a liberating blessing for the world.

23:1 *The Lord is my shepherd,*

I shall not want.

23:2 *He maketh me to lie down in green pastures;*

"I SHALL NOT WANT" does not mean, "I shall not desire," but rather, "I shall not lack." The Hebrew verb *echsar* (lack) is in the future tense, suggesting that freedom from want comes only when you realize that

God is your shepherd. Why? Because it is then that you realize your desires, endless and endlessly unsatisfied, are a distraction seducing you from your true calling and trapping you in the narrow and lifeless worship of the next big thing.

With God as your shepherd, the chains of idolatry are severed. You are now free to be what God is calling you to be: a source of blessing and liberation for the world. David is not saying that with God as your shepherd you will have everything you need to fulfill all your desires, but that you have everything you need to fill God's desire—that you will have everything you need to become a blessing to others by liberating yourself and them from narrowness.

David uses the future tense because he wants you to know that God is not fixed, but flowing; that God does not shepherd you in one moment, but in every moment, and the way you experience God in this moment may not be the way you experience God in the next. God is forever unfolding. God is forever fresh and surprising. So the tools you need to effect liberation are also unfolding, fresh, and surprising. Nothing of God and nothing that is godly is fixed, and slavery is precisely the brutal effort to dam the flow of God and godliness by restricting the flow of freedom and creativity. This is why pharaohs of all kinds and in all ages see themselves as gods. Pharaohs deny God, the unconditioned and unconditional source of all reality, and impose slavery—the denial of godliness and the freedom and creativity godliness demands.

David is saying that when you allow God to shepherd you, when you dare to leave the path for the pathless, the known for the unknown, and take upon yourself the challenge of becoming a blessing and a liberator, you can trust God to provide you with the means for being both in this moment and the next.

I shall not want.

23:2 *He maketh me to lie down in green pastures*

He leadeth me beside the still waters

GOD IS SHEPHERDING YOU toward blessing and liberation, and the first step along the way is "to lie down in green pastures." The first step is to rest, to lie down, because the way to blessing and liberation isn't simply an outer journey, but an inner one as well. You cannot set about being a catalyst for blessing and liberation

19

until you know what it is to be blessed and free. So God makes you lie down.

You want to rush on, to reach the goal, to earn a reward for doing God's work, but the *way* is the goal, the journey is the destination, and the reward is the blessing of being free. The gift of blessing and liberation isn't something you give, but something you are. And lying down in green pastures is the first step in recovering who you are and living your life from that realization.

Chances are you've had this experience before. When you were young you relished stretching out on your back: your face pointing skyward, your body cushioned by soft, cool grass. Can you remember the sense of awe and wonder you felt while lying on your back and staring into the sky? Can you remember feeling both small and infinite at the same time? David insists you lie down rather than sit up. He wants you to gaze into the limitless sky and not toward the directional horizon, because sky gazing brings the narrow mind of ego into contact with the spacious mind of God.

At that moment of lying down and gazing upward, you know what the angels know: "the whole earth is full of God's glory" (Isaiah 6:3). At that moment you know that everything is being done and you are not doing it. You realize that God will bless and God will make you free, and you are simply a means to that end and not its cause. When God makes you to lie down in green pastures, it is to fill you with wonder and to reveal that, as small as you are in the grand scheme of things, you are nonetheless an integral part of that scheme, a part needed to bring blessing and liberation to the world.

2:2 He maketh me to lie down in green pastures

He leadeth me beside the still waters.

2:3 He restoreth my soul:

GOD LEADS YOU from pastures to riverbank, from land to water, from lying down to walking upright, from the wonder revealed in the transcendent sky to the humility taught by still waters—not water that is unmoving, but water that is powerfully flowing, yet tranquil.

Water can be still, raging, or stagnant. Raging waters can break the bonds that enslave you, but they may drown you in the process. Freed too abruptly, you cannot adjust to freedom and, like the newly liberated Hebrews, you rush from the unknown God of Exodus to the familiar worship of Egypt's Golden Calf.

Stagnant water is often unhealthy and not to be drunk. God, by contrast, is *mikor mayim chayyim*, the fountain of living water (Jeremiah 2:13). There is nothing stagnant in God. This is why God defines divinity as *Ehyeh asher Ehyeh*, "I will be whatever I will be" (Exodus 3:14). God is not fixed or stagnant; God is the ever-flowing, ever-changing creativity that manifests as life in all its glory.

Neither the raging nor the stagnant can achieve the liberation God desires. For this we must turn to the still. The phrase "still waters" (*may m'nukhot*) refers to water that is deep and ever-flowing. Still waters seek the low places and flow into the sea. When faced with obstacles, still waters go around or over them. Still waters slowly, calmly, and relentlessly soften the hard edges of all they encounter.

God, like still waters, brings you to the low places, the places of humility. God, like still waters, rolls on, over, and around anything that seeks to dam its flow. God, like still waters, softens you over time. And humility, perseverance, and softening—along with wonder—are the first gifts you receive as you become the vehicle for blessing and liberation God intends you to be.

He leadeth me beside the still waters.

23:3 *He restoreth my soul;*

He leadeth me in the paths of righteousness

WHEN DAVID SPEAKS OF "soul," or *nefesh*, he isn't refer-ring to an immortal spark or personal essence separate from your mortal self. It will be centuries before Jews begin to think in those terms. For David, nefesh refers to *nefesh chayyah*, a living being (Genesis 2:7). When he tells you that God restores your soul, David is saying that God is returning you to your original nature.

What is your original nature? You are *tzelem elohim*, the image of God (Genesis 1:27), a bearer of God's breath, God's spirit: "Then the Ineffable One formed the earthling (*adam*) from the dust of the earth (*adamah*), and breathed the breath of life into its nostrils, and the earthling became a living being (*nefesh chayyah*) (Genesis 2:7).

23

What does it mean to be a breath-bearer? It means to breathe life into the world as God breathed life into you. This is what the Torah reveals when she tells us, "The Ineffable One placed the earthling in the Garden of Eden to till it and protect it" (Genesis 2:15). The garden is the original state of creation, but without you, the earth grows hard and lifeless, incapable of birthing plants or herbs (Genesis 2:5). You must till the garden; you must break up the hard and lifeless patches; you must help the garden breathe; you are the breath-bearer.

But tilling the garden is only half your task; you must also protect it. Protect it from what? From the arrogance and greed of humankind, from those who have forgotten they are the earth's servants rather than her masters. Protect it how? By reminding humanity of its original nature as the image of God and bearers of divine spirit. This remembrance is key to the blessing and liberation you are called to bring into the world.

❄️

23:3 He restoreth my soul.

He leadeth me in the paths of righteousness for His names sake

23:4 Yea, though I walk through the valley

TO UNDERSTAND the meaning of this verse you must begin at the end and work your way backward from "His name's sake" through "paths of righteousness" to "leadeth."

The Name to which David refers is the Ineffable Name of God (Y–H–V–H), the meaning of which is *Ehyeh asher Ehyeh,* "I will be what I will be" (Exodus 3:14). God is ever-flowing being: what was, is, and will be. There is, the Torah tells us, nothing other than God (Deuteronomy 4:35), so when David says God acts for "His Name's sake," he is not saying that God acts for self-aggrandizement, but that God acts on behalf of all reality, for God is all reality.

Understanding this, you can now understand "paths of righteousness." A path is righteous if walking it breathes life into life, if it blesses and benefits creation, and if it fosters love, justice, and compassion.

If it doesn't, it isn't. Each moment of your life you are called to choose: "I set before you life and death, blessing and curse. Choose life . . ." (Deuteronomy 30:19). If you choose life, the path revealed is righteous. If you choose death, the path revealed is unrighteous.

David is identifying a new relationship with God based not on control but on freedom. He signals this change in two ways. First, he changes verbs, a fact our English translation fails to note. When referring to still waters, David uses the verb *nahal*, "to lead," but when speaking of "paths of righteousness," he uses the verb *nachan*, "to gift." From this moment on God leads through gifting: that is, God leads by gifting you with the freedom to follow or not.

for His names sake.

23:4 *Yea, though I walk through the valley of the shadow of death,*

I will fear no evil for Thou art with me;

THE VALLEY SHADOWED BY DEATH is none other than life itself. From the moment of your birth, the possibility and inevitability of death engulfs you. The shadow of death—the fact of your own mortality—is ever-present. There is no escaping this valley or the shadow that darkens it. God doesn't shepherd you around the valley, but through it. In this there is no choice.

Death is not opposed to God's plan; on the contrary, death is essential to it. Death keeps life from becoming stagnant. Death keeps you from becoming complacent. Without death there would be no room for new life. Without death the future would simply mirror the past. Without death God is no longer the fluid "I will be" but the fixed and stagnant "I am."

Death is intrinsic to change, and change is intrinsic to life, and both are a part of God. Death and life are of a single piece, and neither can exist without the other. They define one another, complete one another, and balance one another. And they both play their roles within the larger reality of God.

With God as your shepherd the valley reveals her green pastures and still waters. With God as your shepherd the valley becomes the place of your soul's restoration. With God as your shepherd the valley is where you are gifted with choice and blessing. The valley of the shadow of death is the reality you navigate from moment to moment. There is no way around it, so God shepherds you through it. But do not imagine that "through" means "out." David never mentions an end to the valley. There is no exit except the final one when the shadow of death is breeched by the embrace of death itself.

of the shadow of death,

I will fear no evil for Thou art with me;

Thy rod and Thy staff they comfort me.

WHAT IS THE EVIL no longer feared? It cannot be the everyday tragedies of life—disappointments, old age, illness, or death—for these are part of your walk, even with God as your shepherd. The evil no longer feared is the debilitating sense of anxiety and hopelessness arising from believing the lie that you walk the valley alone.

When you walk alone through the valley of the shadow of death, a terrible pall spreads over you, and your capacity for love is eclipsed by your fear of death. Engulfed by death's shadow you wall yourself off in a defensive tower you call "life" but which is, in fact, a

28

premature death. To protect yourself from the pain of losing someone you love, you choose to love no one at all. Your fear of losing love renders you incapable of loving or being loved.

But when you walk with God, you walk without fear. When you walk without fear, you allow for vulnerability and cultivate love. When you walk with God, death is no less but love is much more. Love is, as David's son Solomon wrote, "as strong as death" (*Song of Songs* 8:6), but not everyone is capable of seeing this.

Walking with God takes many forms. It may mean walking in the presence of an Other, someone or something greater than yourself. It may mean walking shoulder to shoulder with those who suffer, helping them to lighten their load or to carry their burdens more effectively. It may mean working to change the system such that "justice will roll like a might river" (*Amos* 5:24). And it may be a combination of these and more. What marks the spiritual path is not necessarily an other-worldly sense of the supernatural, but a this-worldly awareness of and love for the natural.

The sense of being alone, the notion that you are separate from the whole, apart from God rather than a part of God, is what Albert Einstein called an "optical delusion." Yes, the world as you perceive it looks to be made of this and that, but when you look more closely you see this is a part of that, and that is a part of this, and both are a part of God. You discover there is no alone, and that love grows even in the shadow of death, covering the entire valley with grace.

of the shadow of death,

I will fear no evil **for Thou art with me***;*

Thy rod and Thy staff, they comfort me

SOMETHING EXTRAORDINARY HAPPENS in this line of our psalm: David ceases to speak about God, and begins to speak to God. There is no poetic reason for this shift; there is nothing in the psalm that requires it, but there is something in David that does.

David abruptly changes pronouns from "he" to "you" because his experience of God has changed. He has undergone a shift in consciousness that he wishes you to undergo as well. In the midst of his journey through the valley of the shadow of death, he suddenly realizes he isn't alone. God is there with him; God is here with you.

You may have many ideas about God. You may believe in God or not; you may imagine God to be this or that or the other. But whatever your opinions, they are just that: opinions. As God says to the Prophet Isaiah, "My thoughts are not your thoughts; My ways are not your ways," (*Isaiah* 55:8). God cannot be reduced to isms and ideologies, nor can godliness be reduced to laws and rituals. God can only be met in the immediacy of the moment, and godliness can only arise in the immediacy of that meeting. God is reality—that which is met moment to moment—and godliness is the response to that meeting.

David meets God, his Shepherd, in the valley of the shadow of death. It is a mistake to limit God to the light. A good shepherd walks with the flock, beside the flock. What they confront, the shepherd confronts; their dangers are the shepherd's dangers. It is because the Shepherd is with you that you walk without fear. Not that tragedies won't happen, but that you will not face them alone. This is what David realizes, and why he suddenly stops speaking about God, and begins speaking to God: "Thou art with me." This is why Psalm 23 is the psalm we turn to in moments of grief and sorrow; not because it speaks of some abstract notion of transcendent divinity, but because it seeks to awaken us to the realization of God's shepherding presence in this very moment.

I will fear no evil for Thou art with me,

Thy rod and Thy staff, they comfort me.

Thou preparest a table before me in the

THE SHEPHERD'S ROD is a short stick, perhaps three feet long, with a knob at one end. The shepherd's staff or crook is a long walking stick with a curved top. Together they are the shepherd's essential tools.

The rod helps the shepherd see to the safety and health of the flock. If a lamb is in danger, the shepherd throws the rod toward the danger to ward it off and warn the sheep away. Because wool can hide diseased skin, the shepherd uses the rod to part the wool and see to the health of the skin beneath. God's rod does the same: warning you of dangers ahead, revealing what is beneath the surface so that you can take action to enhance health and well-being.

The staff has many uses. It is a defensive weapon against any who threaten the safety of the flock. It helps the shepherd maintain balance on uneven terrain. It gently lifts and carries a newborn lamb to its mother if they become separated, preventing the scent of the shepherd's hands from causing the mother to reject her lamb. By extending the staff like a guardrail, the shepherd prevents injury as the sheep move along dangerous terrain. It pulls sheep out of deep water and frees them from brambles. And it is used to count the flock as each animal is caused to pass under the shepherd's staff as a sign of coming under the shepherd's protection. God's staff represents those signs and insights that guide you to safety and free you from entrapments.

The shepherd's rod and staff are symbols of care, concern, safety, and liberation. When you are helped out of a crisis, when you are warned of danger or disease, you encounter God's rod and staff. And when you warn and help others, you become God's rod and staff. This is where Psalm 23 is taking you: God is your shepherd leading you through life to restore you to your true self, as the image of God, that you might walk without fear to bring comfort, blessing, and liberation to all you meet.

❧❦

23:5 ***Thou preparest a table before me in the
presence of mine enemies,***

WHAT IS THIS TABLE God sets before you? You may, as many do, imagine this table is a banquet prepared for you to taunt your enemies, but David says nothing about a banquet. This is a not a table for feasting or an opportunity for taunting; this is a table for meeting and an opportunity for reconciliation.

The table God prepares for you in the midst of the valley of the shadow of death is the "land" toward which God called Abraham and Sarah. The enemies who will sit with you are the pharaohs God sent Moses to confront. This is the place toward which God has been shepherding you all along. If you are going to be a blessing, it must happen here with your enemies. If you are going to be a liberator, it is those locked in the narrow place of opposition that you must first set free.

David makes this clear by calling his enemies *tzorrai*, "my narrows," or "those who narrow me." The

34

Hebrew root word here is *tzar*, "narrow." This is also the root of *Mitzrayim*, "Egypt." The enemy is anything that narrows, constricts, or enslaves you or others, anything that denies and diminishes your true nature as the image of God. These are the forces you are to meet at this table.

The table is "before" you, meaning you must walk toward it and take your place. It is set up and in the "presence of" (literally *neged*, "across from") your enemies, meaning that they too must move toward the table if true meeting is to happen. Are the enemies also being shepherded by God? Or are they responding to your willingness to meet? Either way, what David is saying is this: the purpose of God's shepherding is to lead you to the table of meeting where you will confront the powers of narrowness with the command of liberation.

What do you do at this table of meeting? David doesn't say. Indeed, he cannot say, for there is no script for authentic encounter; there can be no formula for liberating self and other. This is both the hope and the horror of the table of meeting. Hope, because it holds out the promise of liberation; horror, because it does not provide a means for achieving it.

35

True meeting happens in that place of not-knowing, that place where you cannot hide behind past hurts or present fears, but must come out of hiding and be present to what is. And what is is always another suffering soul, another person (or perhaps another aspect of yourself) that is trapped, broken, fearful, and longing for love. When you meet the other and see her or his vulnerability, you discover your own, as well. Suddenly there is nothing to fear or defend; there are only tears to shed and broken hearts to mend. If you dare to take your place at this table, you will know what to do.

presence of mine enemies,

Thou anointest my head with oil,

my cup runneth over

THERE ARE ONLY TWO reasons why one's head is anointed with oil in the Hebrew Bible: daily hygiene and becoming king. Each has its own verb, and David makes it clear through his choice of verbs that he is referring to hygiene rather than kingship (*deshan* rather than *mashach*).

In ancient times, as today, people would apply oil to their skin after a bath, and again during the day to protect themselves from the drying effects of the sun and hot desert winds. In our psalm, God anoints your head as you approach the table to meet with your enemies. Speaking metaphorically, David is saying that if you dare to sit at the table God prepares for you, God will protect you from the heat of anger and the soul-drying winds of fear.

How does God do this? Through your realization that God is with you, that you are God's image called to be God's rod and staff by bearing God's breath into the world and by being a source of blessing and liberation to those who are trapped in narrowness. Knowing that God is with you, you take your place at the table with your enemies—inner and outer—and begin to dialogue with them, to understand them, to negotiate with them so that peace can be achieved.

Peace is the ultimate gift of being shepherded by God, but peace doesn't mean the absence of either conflict or suffering. Peace, *shalom*, is linked to *shalem*, wholeness. True peace is the capacity to embrace and engage the whole of life—the good and the bad, the hallowed and the horrifying—without losing your

balance, without locking yourself in the tower of love-
less invulnerability. True shalom comes with the realization that God is with you, inside and out.

Thou anointest my head with oil;

my cup runneth over.

24 Surely goodness and mercy shall follow me all

WHEN THE OIL OF GOD cools the fever of fear, your
cup overflows: you are ready to meet with your enemies and to move beyond narrowness and slavery to
spaciousness and liberation. As with the table mistaken for a banquet, the overflowing cup is often mistaken for a sign of material wealth and abundance.
Somehow this deep and comforting psalm, this call
to remember your true nature and reclaim your inti-
macy with God, is reduced to a tasteless flaunting of
financial success. This is not David's message at all.

This cup is your life. When you allow God to
shepherd you to this table of meeting, when you are
willing to engage with your enemies—confront narrowness and work toward liberation—your life overflows; a new spiritual abundance is triggered. Without

fear, you are suddenly alive to endless possibilities for reconciliation, connection, joy, compassion, and love. This is your cup overflowing.

It is vital that you see Psalm 23 for what it is: not a celebration of one man's fortune, but a call to triumph over fear and existential loneliness, to realize that God is with you always, and, in so doing, to make of yourself a vehicle of blessing and liberation for all the families of the earth.

Where does the overflow of your cup go? What is true of a real cup spilling its contents is true of David's metaphoric cup of life: the spillage is always downward. Like the still waters in verse two, your cup spills into the low places that water prefers. God is shepherding you into the shadowed worlds of the fearful and oppressed, those who are unaware of the shepherding hand of God, unwilling to share a table with their enemies, and still suffering under the mistaken notion that they are alone. Your overflowing cup flows downward to these lost and fearful souls, calling you to walk with them as God walks with you, and in this way, show them the table of meeting and reconciliation, and the hope that such meeting and reconciliation promises.

❊❊❊

my cup runneth over.

23.6 ***Surely goodness and mercy shall follow me***
***all the days of my life**, and I will dwell*

the house of the Lord for ever.

DAVID IS A POET OF GENIUS and he chooses his words
carefully, yet many read this psalm incorrectly: "goodness and mercy shall be with me all the days of my
life." But this is not at all what David says.

Goodness and mercy, David says, shall *follow* you.
Goodness and mercy are behind you not beside you.
Goodness and mercy are not only gifts you receive,
but gifts you bestow. Goodness and mercy are the
wake your life journey leaves behind when you allow
God to shepherd you.

Like Abraham and Sarah, you are called to be a
blessing to all the families of the earth. The blessing
is twofold. For those who dare to listen to your story,
and through your story to discover for themselves the
shepherding hand of God, you bring liberation from
fear and anger, and the opportunity to make of themselves a blessing. For those who are not yet ready to

be free, who cannot accept the fierce comfort of God's rod and staff, who seek to escape from the valley of the shadow of death rather than boldly traverse it, who refuse to sit with their enemies and receive the soothing oil of God, you still have a blessing to leave: goodness and mercy.

Shepherded by God, your life is a cup overflowing, spilling the wisdom you have gleaned to the lowest and narrowest of places. You are not called to escape the valley of the shadow of death, but to return to it over and over and over again to assist others on their journey through it. And as you return and assist, you leave behind goodness and mercy.

Goodness and mercy are the signs of your having passed through the lives of others. They are how you know you are living under the shepherding hand of God. Don't imagine that spirituality cannot be measured, or that living a spiritual life is somehow unrelated to the life you live in the world. On the contrary: living spiritually is how you live in the world.

Living spiritually means living in a manner that cultivates justice, compassion, and humility (Micah 6:8), both within yourself and between yourself and others. If knowing you brings mercy and goodness

41

into people's lives, you are walking with God. If knowing you brings needless pain and suffering into people's lives, you are walking alone.

2:6b *Surely goodness and mercy shall follow me all the days of my life,* ***and I will dwell*** *in the house of the Lord for ever.*

WHAT DOES DAVID MEAN by *shavti*, "I will dwell?" The Hebrew root word is *sh-v-t* from which we derive the noun *Shabbat* and the verb "to cease from work." When David says we dwell in the House of God, he is not referring to where we live but to how we live. To dwell in the House of God is to cease working at life, and to begin working with it.

When you work *at* life you seek to impose your will *on* life. Your standard of right and wrong, good and bad, righteous and unrighteous becomes nothing more than your own will, whim, and desire. You are pleased when things go your way, and displeased when they don't. Most often, however, life goes against your desires. There are tragedies you don't want, illness you'd rather avoid, pain and suffering that, if life were up to you, would not exist. But they do exist. Like it or not, will it or not, desire it or not, you walk through the valley of the shadow of death. You have no choice.

The only choice you do have is whether to walk fearfully or fearlessly. Psalm 23 is a guide to walking without fear. When you do, you no longer seek to impose what should be, but learn to work with what is, and to do so gracefully, effortlessly, and without coercion of self or others. Working with life means accepting what is—in order to change what is next. If you want peace, you must first accept the fact of conflict. If you want to turn your enemies into friends, you must first sit down with them as enemies.

This is another meaning to David's opening teaching: when you realize God is your shepherd, you shall not want things to be other than they are. On the contrary, you will engage things just as they are, and do so for the sake of blessing and liberation, leaving only goodness and mercy in your wake.

❧❧

all the days of my life, and I will dwell
in the House of the Lord for ever.

WHERE IS THE HOUSE OF GOD? The House of God is where God dwells, yet is there a place God does not dwell? The angels tell us the whole earth is filled with God's glory (*Isaiah* 6:3). Our sages tell us "there is no place devoid of God" (*Tikkunei Zohar*, 57), that God fills and surrounds all worlds (*Zohar* III: 225a), that God "is the life of all that lives" (*Hymn of Glory*), that "everything is in God, and God is in everything and beyond everything, and there is nothing other than God" (*Elimah Rabbati* 24d-25a). Even the inanimate is not other than God: "Do not say a rock is a rock and not God, for all existence is God, and the rock is a thing filled with God . . . God is found in everything, and there is nothing besides God" (*Perek Helek*, 206b). The House of God, then, is reality itself. Unfortunately, too many have forgotten this, imagining instead that God's House is anywhere but here, when in fact it can be nowhere but here.

Psalm 23 is a call to remembering. What David is saying is this:

44

If you realize that God is your shepherd; if you allow God to lay you down in green pastures and lead you beside still waters; if you walk with God through the valley of the shadow of death, if you dare to sit at the table of meeting and reconcile with your enemies, if you cool your anger and cease to fear, if you follow the overflow of your cup and reach out to the lowest and the least, then your life will be a blessing to those who are lost, a catalyst for liberation among those who are enslaved, and you will leave goodness and mercy in your wake. When you do all this, you will discover that you have been and always will be living in the House of God.

*all the days of my life, and I will dwell in the House of the Lord **for ever**.*

THE VERY END of our Psalm is two words in Hebrew: *orech yamim*, long days. Long days are not the same as forever. If David had meant to say "forever" he would have written *l'olam*, but he wrote *orech yamim* instead. Why?

Days seem long or short depending on your state of mind, and, unfortunately in English, days we call "long days" are usually days filled with strife and suffering. But what is true of English is not true of Hebrew. *Orech yamim* are days overflowing as your cup overflows; to David's mind, long days are days filled with life so abundant that they seem to spill over, breaking the boundaries of actual time and lifting you into a sense of timelessness.

Chances are you have had such overflowing days—days when you were so engrossed in what you were doing that time stopped, and you were filled with a nameless joy bordering on and perhaps even passing into ecstasy. This is what it is to live in the House of God.

Dwelling in God's House is not a reward for living this overflowing life; it is this overflowing life. Yet not every day is lived in ecstasy, nor is the experience of ecstasy the only or primary hallmark of living in the House of God. We live in God's house when we live with the preciousness of each moment; when, no matter how difficult our situation or how great our loss or deep our pain, we sense something more, something greater than loss, something we might call love.

Not love in the romantic sense, but love in the sense of expansiveness, a love that takes us through our suffering to something greater, something consoling.

Even our greatest grief is a sign of love, for if we did not love what we have lost, we would feel no grief. Our mourning is not simply a sign of our having lost, but an affirmation of our having dared to love.

AFTERWORD

I APPROACHED THIS GUIDE to the 23rd Psalm with much trepidation. To work with such an iconic text, and to do so in a way that would enrich its meaning for those who already cherish it, is daunting to say the least. I will leave it to you to judge whether and to what extent I have succeeded. What I want to share in these final pages is what I learned in the process.

First, there is no such thing as a simple biblical text. I have read the 23rd Psalm hundreds of times as a rabbi, a student of biblical literature, and a spiritual seeker, yet as I worked with the text for this small book, I discovered a psalm far more intellectually challenging and spiritually compelling than I had hitherto known it to be. My familiarity with the text had caused me to forget the radical nature of its message. Knowing the words by heart, I had failed to take them to heart. Writing this book changed that for me.

Second, there is no such thing as a dead biblical text. As I read and reread Psalm 23, it began to speak to me in new and unexpected ways: ways that called me to a deeper encounter with God, the Source and Substance of all Reality. "The Lord is my shepherd" is David's metaphor and David's experience. But as the psalm took hold of me, it became my experience and my metaphor as well. The more the psalm took hold of me, the more I felt the rod and staff of God comforting me.

Third, there is no such thing as a definitive translation of a biblical text. All translation is commentary; in moving from Hebrew to English, the translator is relying on theology as much as, if not more than, linguistics. For example, when rendering God's Name as *Lord*, the translator introduces issues of gender, politics, and power that the Name itself does not intend. God is *Ehyeh asher Ehyeh*, "I will be whatever I will be" (Exodus 3:14): intrinsically unconditioned and unconditionable, and so very different from the "Lord" so often flaunted by the powerful for their own political gain. To be shepherded by David's God is not to be led along conventional paths, but along the pathless land that only God can show you (Genesis 12:1).

The 23rd Psalm is both a call and a challenge. It calls you to realize that God, Reality, is shepherding you through life, what David calls the "valley of the shadow of death," toward the table of reconciliation. It challenges you to take your place at that table, to engage your enemies—those people, places, relationships, obligations, etc., that narrow, constrict, and enslave—in a way that leads to an abundance of blessing and liberation so effervescent that it spills over and seeps downward to the lowest and narrowest of places. The 23rd Psalm reveals the Way of God.

The Way of God is the watercourse way seeking the low and the humble. The Way of God is the way of blessing and liberation. The Way of God is the way of righteousness, justice, and compassion that leaves only goodness and mercy in its wake. The Way of God is not a fixed path, a paved road, but a pathless land, a way unmapped and unchartered either by the past or by conventions that too often sanctify that which is only sanctimonious. The Way of God, the Way recounted by David in this his greatest of psalm, is the Way to which Abram and Sarai were called, the Way to which Moses was called, the Way to which you are called, the Way to which all are called who dare to place themselves under the shepherding rod and staff of Reality.

I believe David wrote this psalm by himself but not for himself. He meant it to call each of us out of our narrowness and into our destiny. He meant it to humble us, and free us to walk the low places dark with death's shadow, and in this way, to bring the light of blessing and freedom to all we meet.

Let me close this brief glimpse into my reading of the 23rd Psalm with my personal recasting of it, not as an alternative to the original, but as a complement.

A Psalm of David

23:1 *Reality alone shepherds me,*
simplifying my needs and fulfilling them.

23:2 *Lying in green pastures,*
I know the One who is all. Walking beside still
waters,
I humbly follow the watercourse way.

23:3 *My soul is restored;*
I remember I am the image of God.
When I walk Your path—righteous, just, and
compassionate,
I act not for myself, but for the welfare of all.

23:4 *When I walk through life's valley shadowed*
by death,
I fear no separation for You are with me;
Your rod warns me of danger,
Your staff alerts me to dis-ease.

23:5 *You set before me a table of meeting where*
I encounter all that enslaves me,
within and without.
You cool my anger,
Your blessings overflow, bringing liberation to
the lowest places.

23:6 *When I walk with You*
I leave only goodness and mercy in my wake.
When I take refuge in You,
I know every place is Your place, and every
face is Your face.
Time ceases, death no longer strangles love,
I walk with fierce and freeing faith the pathless
land to which You summon me.

CHAPTER TWO

Jesus' Two Great Commandments

THE 23RD PSALM is not the only touchstone text in the Bible. Indeed, there are as many such texts as there are people to be touched by them. I chose Psalm 23 because it is just such a meaningful text for so many. I chose Jesus' teaching of the Two Great Commandments because these two commandments were touchstones for him.

I want you to hear this: When Jesus is asked to reveal the essential commandments (*mitzvot*, as he would have called them) of the spiritual life, he could have said, "I am the resurrection and the life. Whoever lives and believes in me will never die" (John 11:25). Or he could have said, "Truly, truly, I say to you, unless you are born again, you cannot see the Kingdom of God" (John 3:3). Or he could have said, "I am the light of the world; you who follow me shall not walk in darkness, but shall have the light of life" (John 8:12). Or he could have said, "Truly, truly, I say unto you, if any of you keeps my word you will never see death" (John 8:51). But he didn't say any of these things, or even anything remotely like them. He didn't reference himself at all.

Instead, he cited two texts from the Torah, Deuteronomy 6: 4–5 and Leviticus 19:18, and taught that the central commandments are to love God and love your neighbor. When asked to reveal the way people can realize their connection with God and live out their lives in a godly manner, which is what the word *mitzvah* (*mitzvot*, plural) means, Jesus quoted these two texts from the Torah—the Bible as he knew it. Why these to and not some others? There can be but one answer: these two texts are the touchstone teachings of Jesus; these two texts are the texts he himself must have turned to in his own life.

Here are the two versions of this Gospel story starting with Mark, which is the older of the two and which is most likely the source for Matthew's version:

Gospel According to
Mark 12:28–34

One of the rabbis came near and ... asked
Jesus, "Which mitzvah is the most important?"
Jesus answered, "There are two. The first is,
Hear, O Israel: the Lord our God, the Gospel
According to Mark 12: 28–34. *Lord is one; you*
shall love the Lord your God with all your heart,
and with all your soul, and with all your mind,
and with all your strength. The second is this:
You shall love your neighbor as yourself. There
is no other mitzvah greater than these." Then
the rabbi said to him, "You are right, Rabbi;
you have truly said that *he is one, and besides*
him there is no other; and *to love him with all*
the heart, and with all the understanding, and
with all the strength, and *to love one's neighbor*
as oneself is much more important than all the
burnt offerings and sacrifices." When Jesus saw
that he answered wisely, he said to him, "You
are not far from the kingdom of God." After
that no one dared to ask him any question.
(*My translation*)

55

The Gospel According to
Matthew 22:34–40

When the Pharisees heard that Jesus had
silenced the Sadducees, they gathered together,
and one of them, a rabbi, asked him a question
to test him. "Rabbi, which of the Torah's
mitzvot is the greatest?" Jesus said to him,
"You shall love *Adonai* (the Lord) your God
with all your heart, and with all your soul, and
with all your mind. This is the greatest and
first mitzvah. And the second is like it, "You
shall love your neighbor as yourself." On these
two mitzvot hang the Torah and Prophets. (*My
translation*)

Think about this for a moment: Where else in the
Gospels is Jesus asked to share what he believes to be
the heart of his faith? There are many places, especially in the Gospel According to John, where Jesus
speaks to his relationship with God and his sense of
self and mission here on earth, and these have become
touchstones for many people. But they were not and
could not be touchstones for Jesus because they didn't
exist until Jesus spoke them.

And while it is true that Jesus often comments on other verses of the Hebrew Bible, adding his unique insights to them and often shifting their meaning in significant ways, as he does when using the teaching of "an eye for an eye" (Exodus 21:23-25) to introduce his notion that one should not resist evil (Matthew 5:38–39), none of these texts is a touchstone for him. On the contrary, they are texts he wants to challenge and change, not ones that he uses to guide his life and the lives of others. For this purpose he chooses to speak of loving God and neighbor.

What Jesus offers us with these touchstones is his deepest understanding of his religion. Indeed, these two passages cited by Jesus as the greatest of the Torah's mitzvot express the religion of Jesus. This is the Judaism in which he himself believed.

The religion *of* Jesus is very different from the religion *about* Jesus. The religion of Jesus, like the religion of David, was Judaism as each of these great sages understood it. The religion about Jesus is Christianity. The religion of Jesus never mentions Jesus. The religion about Jesus is nothing without him.

I admit to knowing very little regarding the religion about Jesus. That I leave to Christians. And while

I am always curious, and enjoy sitting with Christians and listening to their experiences of and with Christ, I always do so as an outsider for I have no such experiences of my own.

When it comes to the religion of Jesus, however, I am, as Jesus was, a rabbi, and hence steeped in the same spiritual path. Not only that, but in this case I am also a follower of Rabbi Jesus, for I, too, affirm the unity and love of God and the love of humanity as the essential teaching of Judaism. For me, for most Jews, and for our fellow Jew, Rabbi Jesus, Deuteronomy 6: 4–5 and Leviticus 19:18 are touchstone texts.

I suspect that most readers of Matthew and Mark, and most readers of this *Guide* are not rabbis or even Jews. I suspect that for most of you, Jesus as Christ rather than the Torah is your touchstone. And because I think this is true, I fear you may overlook some of the deeper insights Jesus meant to teach when he chose these two mitzvot as the chief commandments of the Torah and his touchstone texts. It is my wish to make plain the deeper meaning of his teaching by placing it in the Jewish context in which it was spoken by Jesus and heard by his fellow Jews, and in this way enhance your understanding of Jesus' message.

THE SETTING

Jesus lived in first-century, Roman-occupied Jewish Palestine. It was a time of brutal oppression and it was this oppression and occupation that defined the four major factions that dominated Jewish life in that time: the Sadducees, Pharisees, Essenes, and Zealots. Each had its own approach to Roman occupation: collaborate, separate, isolate, and liberate, respectively. Let's take up each group in turn.

SADDUCEES

Taking their name from the family of Tzadok, an ancient High Priest, the Sadducees comprised the upper crust of Judean society. They were the leaders of finance as well as religion. While not all Sadducees were priests, almost all priests were Sadducees. To maintain their position and power the Sadducees learned to collaborate with Rome. In their mind, what was good for Rome was good for the Sadducees, and what was good for the Sadducees was good for Rome.

The Sadducees believed in the centrality of the Jewish Temple and its sacrifices. For them Judaism was the Temple, and being an observant Jew meant participating in the rites and rituals of the Temple, over which the Sadducees had complete control. There was no Judaism without the Temple, and there could not be Temple without the priests. And the survival of all three—Judaism, Temple, and priesthood—depended on the good graces of Rome.

Rome was primarily concerned with the collection of taxes. As long as the money came into Caesar's treasury, Caesar was happy and the Jews survived. If the money stopped coming in, Rome would send her soldiers to see that whatever was causing the stoppage was removed. Removal meant death, usually by crucifixion.

Caiaphas was the Roman appointed High Priest at the time of Jesus, a position he managed to hold longer than any of his predecessors. This was no small feat and attests to his genius as a politician. In the New Testament, Caiaphas is central to the opposition to Jesus, an idea not hard to believe. Jesus upset the status quo, while Caiaphas' power, position, and perhaps even his life depended upon maintaining it. When Jesus challenged the ruling class, both Jewish and Roman, to live up to the Torah's call for justice; when he pitted the Kingdom of Rome against the Kingdom of God; and when his disciples denied Caesar's claim to be the Son of God and instead put forth a Jew from Galilee, Caiaphas could only have acted as he did. Jesus was a threat that had to be eliminated. If he failed to do so, Rome would do it for him, and probably remove him as well. And, as we all know, while Caiaphas may have been a catalyst for the death of Jesus, it was Rome and Rome alone that had the power to execute him.

PHARISEES

The word Pharisee comes from the Hebrew *parush*, "to set apart," and speaks to the Pharisaic attempt to create a separate society alongside that of the Sadducees, one that minimized its contact with Rome as much as possible. The tension this created can be seen in the story of Jesus' teaching on "rendering to Caesar what is Caesar's."

Jesus had been preaching a parable that highlighted the injustice of the priests and Sadducees. His popularity among the people made it impossible for them to harm him, so they sought to put him in a Catch-22 situation where he would either anger his fans or anger the Romans.

> Then they sent some Pharisees and some
> Herodians to Jesus in order to trap him in

61

what he said. And they came and said to him, "Rabbi, we know that you are righteous, and show no preference to anyone, and treat all people equally, and in this way you teach the way of God in accordance with truth. So we would like to ask you a question: Is it lawful to pay taxes to Caesar, or not? Should we pay them, or should we not?"

Seeing through their flattery and knowing their hypocrisy, he said to them, "Why waste your time testing me? Bring me a denarius and let me see it." And they brought one. Then he said to them, "Whose head is this, and whose title?" They answered, "Caesar's."

Jesus said to them, "Then render unto Caesar what is Caesar's, and unto God what is God's." And they were utterly amazed at him. (Mark 12:13–17)

62

Let me go into this story momentarily to help us understand what Jesus is doing. To put it simply, Jesus never really answers the question. He could not answer it. As his enemies rightly understood, any answer would be his undoing. If he said "yes, pay taxes to Rome," those followers who hoped Jesus would free them of the oppressive taxation of Rome would have left him. If he had said "no, don't pay your taxes," the soldiers of Rome would have imprisoned and crucified him. So Jesus answered in a different way. First he revealed the hypocrisy of these particular Pharisees, and then he left the question of paying taxes open to debate. Let me show you how.

Remember the Pharisees were a movement that prided itself on avoiding contact with Rome as much as possible. The Sadducees, against whom Jesus had been preaching just prior to our story, sent "some Pharisees and Herodians" to catch Jesus in a political trap. The word "some" here is crucial.

Sadducees and Pharisees did not get along. Jesus, as we shall see, was most likely a Pharisee himself, hence his preaching against the Temple and its priesthood, who he saw as collaborating with Rome in the oppression and exploitation of the Jews. The only Pharisees that the Sadducees could send to do their bidding were those already marginalized from the Pharisaic movement and in the pocket of the Sadducees. Along with these hypocrites (essentially Sadducean lackeys in Pharisaic clothing), they send

63

some Herodians—officials of King Herod, a lackey of Rome whose job it was to keep the Jews in line and quell any possible rebellion. The Pharisees were sent so that if Jesus said Jews should pay their taxes, these Pharisees would foment against Jesus as a collaborator no better than the Sadducees. The Herodians were sent so that if Jesus said Jews should not pay their taxes, these Herodians could report back to Herod who would, with the blessing of Rome, arrest Jesus and turn him over to the Romans as a political prisoner.

The Pharisees address Jesus as "rabbi," a sign of respect among fellow Pharisees. We see the same thing in both versions of the Two Great Commandments. The Pharisees hope to use flattery to lull Jesus into complacency, but calling him rabbi would not have done that. If he wasn't a rabbi, calling him one would not have flattered him. If he wasn't part of the Pharisaic school, and all rabbis were Pharisees, linking him to it would have been insulting, something these fellows were trying to be. Jesus accepts the title, he is a rabbi, but sees through the rest of their flattery.

Then they put forth their dangerous question: should Jews pay taxes to Rome or not? Jesus doesn't answer, but asks for a Roman coin. When they hand one over, Jesus has already won the argument. They are not seeking to actually debate the necessity of paying taxes, they are seeking to trap him over whether to collaborate with Rome or not. When they are shown to be carrying Roman currency Jesus has caught them in their own trap. It is they who are Roman collaborators merely by participating in the Roman economic system. Taxes are a minor concern if you are already in bed with the oppressor and his exploitative economic policies.

Jesus asks them whose face is on the coin to make it clear that they are the collaborators, not he. After all, Jesus didn't have a coin. The onlookers are "utterly amazed," not at the non sequitur "render unto Caesar what is Caesar's and unto God what is God's," but at how cleverly Jesus revealed the hypocrisy of his inquisitors.

Non sequitur or not, there is still a bit more to say regarding "render unto Caesar what is Caesar's and unto God what is God's." What is Caesar's? The coins with his face and name on them, so give those back to him. Does this mean Jesus is telling us to pay taxes? Not necessarily. He could simply and dangerously be saying, "Don't participate in the exploitative Roman

65

economy." As for returning to God what is God's, the message is simple: "The earth is God's" (Psalm 24:1).

Knowing that the earth belongs to God puts an end to the notion that it can be owned by landlords. In Jesus' time most people had lost their ancestral lands to absentee landlords who then leased the land back to them at exorbitant prices. In effect they were forced into debt as they strove to make a living. This was part and parcel of the Roman economic system, and it is most likely that Jesus is attacking this system. Not only are these Pharisees in the pocket of the Sadducees who are in turn in the pocket of their Roman over-lords, but the entire Kingdom of Rome—based as it is on military power and punitive justice (punishing the poor for the benefit of the rich, punishing the lib-erators for the benefit of the occupiers)—is an affront to the Kingdom of God: the stark alternative, based on compassion and distributive justice that sees to the empowerment and well-being of all people, where every person sits under her own vine and fig tree no longer afraid that it will be confiscated by the govern-ment (Micah 4:4).

This is essentially the radical view of the biblical Prophets, which became part of the political platform of the Pharisees of which Jesus was, at least during his educational years, a part.

The Pharisees separated themselves from the system of the oppressor, both Rome and Rome's lackeys, as best they could. For example, while they (like Jesus) did not oppose the Temple, they did offer (like Jesus) an alternative to run alongside it; one not rooted in priestly piety and adherence to Temple ritual, but in personal piety and adherence to the Torah as the Pharisees came to understand and teach it. They were at times a social group, a political party, and a religious movement. In general, all three of these overlapped into a single effort to redefine what it was to be Jewish. Unlike the Sadducees, who were largely a pro-Roman aristocracy, the Pharisees were more populist, democratic, and progressive, though the Sadducees would have called them radical.

The Pharisees introduced into Judaism the idea of the Two-Fold Torah (literally, "instruction" not "law"): the Written Torah given by God to Moses on Mount Sinai and contained in the Five Books of Moses, and the Oral Torah also given by God to Moses on Sinai and passed down by word of mouth. According to the opening verse of Pirke Avot, a first-century Pharisaic

67

collection of ethical teachings, "Moses received Torah from Sinai and transmitted it to Joshua; Joshua to the elders; the elders to the prophets; and the prophets handed it down to the men of the Great Assembly (Pirke Avot 1:1). The men of the Great Assembly were the forerunners of the Pharisees, who in turn became the rabbis.

With this single sentence the Pharisees secured their centrality in Jewish life, clearly aligned themselves with the justice message of the prophets, and sidelined the Sadducees by leaving the priests out of their recounting of history; in effect, denying that the Sadducees had the complete revelation from God. While the Written Torah passed from Moses to Aaron, the first priest, and from him to subsequent priests and ultimately into the hands of the Sadducees, the Oral Torah—the teachings needed to understand the meaning of the Written Torah—were never given to Aaron, and its transmission bypassed the priests. While it is true, the Pharisees said, that the Sadducees are heirs to the priesthood of Aaron and thus the rightful functionaries of the Temple, they are not the masters of revelation for they have only the outer form and not the inner intent and meaning.

The Sadducees rejected the Pharisaic history of revelation with its deliberate ignoring of the priesthood in favor of the sages (rabbis), and did not agree with nor feel bound by the rulings of the rabbis. On the contrary, they thought the rabbis to be usurpers.

Unlike the Sadducees, whose Judaism was Temple-centric, the Pharisees' Oral Torah applied Judaism to the everyday life of ordinary men and women. And, unlike the Sadducees whose position was secured largely by birth, the Pharisees took seriously the Torah's claim that Israel was to be a nation of priests. To that end, they created a scholarly meritocracy open to any male with the intellectual capacity to learn the Torah and apply its teachings as the rabbis understood them.

The Pharisaic party was divided into conservative and liberal camps, the former led by the followers of Shammai (50 BCE – 30 CE), the latter by the followers of Hillel (110 BCE – 10 CE). The difference between the two is captured in the following rabbinic legend:

> A gentile came to Shammai and asked to be
> converted to Judaism on the condition that
> Shammai teach him the entire Torah while
> standing on one foot. Outraged at the man's

insolence, Shammai chased him away. The
man then went to Hillel with the same request.
Hillel obliged saying, "What is hateful to you
do not do to another. That is the whole of
Torah; all the rest is commentary. Now go and
study it." (Shabbat 31a)

Shammai was a stickler for law and order; Hillel
saw all of Judaism as an expression of the Golden
Rule. Jesus, if he was a rabbi as the Gospels teach, was
clearly of the school of Hillel.

In the New Testament the Pharisees are often por-
trayed as the enemies of Jesus, and the terms "Pharisee"
and "Pharisaic" are used even in modern discourse
as pejoratives. After two millennia of defamatory
Christian usage, a Pharisee today is a person wedded
to the letter of the law rather than its spirit. The irony
is painful to those, like Jesus and myself, who are
heirs to the Pharisees and know them to be scholars.
It was the Pharisees alone who sought to free people
from the letter of the law and to renew Judaism with
the spiritual insights of their Oral Torah. But, as we
shall see, some of the negativity toward the Pharisees
is based on a misunderstanding of their encounters

with Jesus, especially in the story of the Two Great Commandments.

ESSENES

The word *essenoi*, from which the word Essene comes, signifies holiness. The Essene community saw itself as the holy elect of Israel. They rarely married or had children, possessed no money (avoided any collaboration with the economic system), and lived outside the cities and towns of Judea, primarily in *Ein Gedi*, an oasis near the Dead Sea.

The Essenes believed that their fellow Jews had lost their way, and expected God to send a redeemer who would lead them in a war of liberation against with Rome. They referred to this as the War Between the Children of Light and the Children of Darkness. The redeemer would be their resurrected founder—a man whom they called the Teacher of Righteousness—who died decades earlier.

The Teacher of Righteousness was the first messiah among the Jews, a figure predating Jesus by roughly 100 years. This figure, whom some scholars believe was named Judah, rose to prominence during the reign of the Jewish king, Alexander Jannaeus (103

71

BCE – 76 BCE). A priest, he also served as a confidant to the king.

Judah became dissatisfied with the religious sects in Jerusalem, and in reaction founded a cult of his own claiming he was the fulfillment of various biblical prophecies, with an emphasis on those found in Isaiah, especially the idea of the Suffering Servant of the Lord (Isaiah, Chapter 53).

The Teacher of Righteousness was killed by the religious leadership in Jerusalem, and his followers hailed him as a messianic figure who had been raised up into heaven where he took his place beside the Throne of God. They anticipated that the Teacher would return to judge the wicked and lead the righteous into a golden age. The Essenes took the separatist approach both to Rome and the rest of Jewish society, preparing themselves for the return of their Teacher.

BIRYONIM/SICARII/ZEALOTS

The Zealots were called *biryonim* ("ruffians") by the Jews, and *sicarii* by the Romans. *Sicarii* is Latin for "dagger men," and referred to the fact that the Zealots were terrorists who murdered Roman soldiers whenever possible.

Like the Essenes, the Zealots were messianists expecting a military leader to rise up among the Jews and lead them in a war of liberation against Rome. Unlike the Essenes, who were waiting for their Teacher to return before starting their war against Rome, the Zealots believed that by sparking the war themselves, they would force God's hand and hasten the coming of their military messiah.

Judas Iscariot, or Judas the Daggerman, may have been both a Zealot and a member of Jesus' inner circle. Jesus' teachings about the destruction of the Temple, and his radical views on justice for the poor and the meek might have been seen by some Zealots as just the kind of message their hoped-for messiah would bring. On the other hand, Jesus' notion that his own death was part of the bargain, and his lack of teachings regarding military victory and Judean independence may have led the Zealots to reject him, and Judas to betray him.

Decades after the death of Jesus, the Zealots managed to incite a war against Rome. Their misguided adventure lead to the fall of Jerusalem, the sacking of the Temple, the slaughter of thousands, and the two-thousand-year-long exile of the Jews.

The destruction of the Temple in 70 CE, ended the role of the Sadducees and their Temple priesthood. The failure of the military campaign against Rome weakened the role of the Zealots (though they did spark a second war almost a century later that did further damage to the Jews). And the failure of the Teacher of Righteousness to return did the same for the Essenes. Only the Pharisees survived Roman occupation, leaving them and the emerging Christian Jewish movement to determine how the Word of God would be spread in the world.

A FIFTH RESPONSE: PROPHETIC TRANSFORMATION

It is my belief that Jesus, through his training in the liberal Pharisaic school of Hillel, offers an alternative to the four basic responses to Roman occupation (the collaboration of the Sadducees, the separatism of the Pharisees, the isolationism of the Essenes, and the militarism of the Zealots). I call his response Prophetic Transformation and take as my central text Matthew 5:38 – 39: "You have heard it said, 'An eye for an eye, a tooth for a tooth,' but I say unto you, resist not evil."

The word we translate as "resist" is the Greek *anti-stenai*. This is a military term referring to drawing up battle lines against an enemy. Like the Sadducees, Pharisees, and Essenes, and unlike the Zealots, Jesus knew that his fellow Jews could not defeat Rome on the field of battle. His teaching of "resist not" is not a call to abandon this world in hopes of a better lot in heaven, but a strategic warning not to engage Rome in direct military conflict, and to find more creative ways to defeat the enemy and liberate oneself.

The evidence for this interpretation can be found in the teachings that immediately follow Jesus' call to find a new kind of resistance: "If anyone strikes you on the right cheek, turn the other also" (Matthew 5:39).

Most people who deliberate over this passage focus on the notion of turning the other cheek, and overlook the fact that Jesus actually specifies just which cheek this other cheek is; namely, the left cheek. Why is he so specific?

First, the kind of slap Jesus is talking about is a backhand slap by a right-handed person. In both Jewish and Roman society such a slap is meant to humiliate. Roman soldiers, for example, would arbitrarily backhand Jews as a sign of Roman superiority and a reminder that the Jews were no better than animals. Jewish society, too, understood the pain of such a slap, and the Pharisees legislated against it, fining any Jew who slapped a person with the back of the hand a day's pay (400 *zuz*). To better understand how strongly they felt about such a slap, a punch in the face merited only a 4 zuz fine, and an open-handed slap to the left cheek merited a 200 zuz fine.

Jesus isn't speaking in generalities. He is taking the teachings of his Pharisaic colleagues to a new level. Where they were content to restore the honor of the person who was slapped by levying fines, fines that no one could hope to collect when the person administering the slap was a Roman, Jesus seeks not simply to punish the aggressor but to force him to confront his actions in a way that might actually change his personality.

In other words, Jesus is saying, "If even a Roman demean you with a backhanded slap, do not stand against him in battle, but challenge him to a deeper confrontation by offering him your left cheek; dare him to slap you on the left cheek with his forehand, which, though still a sign of anger is yet a sign of anger between equals." This, of course, the Roman cannot do, for his entire system of oppression rested on his insistence that the Jew was not his equal. Whatever the

Roman's response to your "cheeky" behavior might be, it will result in a spectacle that not only makes plain the absurdity of Roman occupation, but perhaps frees the Roman from the oppressive system by helping him see the occupied as an equal.

Jesus makes a similar point when he says, "If anyone forces you to go one mile, go also the second mile" (Matthew 5: 41). "Anyone," here, is a Roman soldier. Roman occupation law allowed Roman soldiers to force occupied people to function as pack animals for up to one mile. We see this in the Gospels of Mark and Matthew when the Romans force a man named Simon of Cyrene to carry Jesus' cross once Jesus himself is too weak to do so (Mark 15:21, Matthew 27:32).

Jesus is saying, do not resist this law by seeking war against Rome, but do not allow yourself to be demeaned by it either. When the first mile is done, offer to go a second; that is, offer to befriend the very man who sought to reduce you to the status of a mule. The Roman soldier will have to reject the offer, for to accept it would be to recognize that you are his equal, something he cannot do and continue to maintain his power over you. So he will demand the return of his pack, and you will insist upon carrying it for him. As a crowd gathers to see what the fuss is all about, the Roman will be humbled by the attempted friendship of the lowly Jew, as well as the bystanders, and perhaps the Roman soldier will once again be reminded that Jews (and other oppressed people) are no less human than those who dominate them.

These two references to Roman occupation are separated by Jesus' teaching regarding debtor's court: "If anyone sues you and takes your outer garment, give them your under garment as well" (Matthew 5:40). The economy of Roman-occupied Palestine was based on the financial exploitation of the poor to sustain the lifestyles of the wealthy and the military adventures of Caesar. Peasants were driven by desperation into selling their land to pay taxes and buy seed for planting. When their money inevitably ran out they would take out loans using whatever property they had as collateral. For some that meant the very clothes on their back. Poverty was systemic, and the courts were used to strip the poor of what little they had left.

Jesus is saying, if the wealthy and the courts that serve them hold your outer garment as collateral, and then take it from you when you cannot repay your debt, give them your undergarment as well. Exit the court naked, and allow your nakedness to inflame the people to resist the oppressive economics of empire. They will see the benefits of siding with the benevolent Kingdom of God, one intent on distributive justice that restores people to economic independence.

The American experience of Muslim outrage at the stripping of prisoners at Abu Ghraib shows the powerful psychological weapon of enforced nakedness on those forced to endure it. Jesus is drawing on the same sense of injustice and shame. He is holding the court accountable for stripping the people of everything. Standing naked before the court offers compelling testimony of the lengths to which the wealthy (and those who collaborate with them) will go in their abuse of the poor.

The historian and Jesus scholar Walter Wink, in a radio program entitled *The Third Way* (first broadcast on November 14, 1993), sets up Jesus' response to Roman occupation this way:

- Seize the moral initiative;
- Find a creative alternative to violence;

- Assert your own humanity and dignity as a person;
- Meet force with ridicule or humor;
- Break the cycle of humiliation;
- Refuse to submit or to accept the inferior position;
- Expose the injustice of the system;
- Take control of the power dynamic;
- Shame the oppressor into repentance;
- Stand your ground;
- Make the Powers make decisions for which they are not prepared;
- Recognize your own power;
- Be willing to suffer rather than retaliate;
- Force the oppressor to see you in a new light;
- Deprive the oppressor of a situation where a show of force is effective;
- Be willing to undergo the penalty of breaking unjust laws;
- Die to fear of the old order and its rules;
- Seek the oppressor's transformation.

Of course, the oppressor can't be expected to transform easily, especially when the transformation will cost him his status, power, and wealth. He will respond harshly, to which Jesus calls on us to love all the more strongly. In the end the oppressor has but two choices: change in the way Jesus is pushing, or put an end to the agitator. Most will opt for the second alternative, which brings us to the trial and death of Jesus.

If Jesus was, as I am arguing, a rabbi and a member of the liberal Hillel school of Pharisaic Judaism; if he road into Jerusalem to the celebratory cries of a great crowd of Jews waving palm branches and calling, "Hosanna! Blessed is the one who comes in the name of the Lord—the King of Israel" (John 12: 12–13), why did these very same Jews turn on him, demand the release of Barabbas, and call for Jesus' crucifixion? The answer is simple: they didn't.

The Gospels, like all written texts, carry the intent of their authors. Matthew, Mark, Luke, and John each have a story to tell, and often it is not the same story. When it comes to the trial of Jesus, however, the intent of all four Gospel writers is to blame the Jews rather than Pilate for Jesus' death. This makes good marketing sense: if you are trying to differentiate yourself from Jews and Judaism, and bring your message to the larger Roman world, it helps to make the Jews the bad guys and the Romans the hapless good guys. But even the best authors of historical fiction cannot evade the basic facts, and this is no less true of the Gospel writers. The truth of Jesus' trial and the Jews reaction to it is buried in the Gospels themselves, specifically in the story of Barabbas.

We are told in the New Testament and the non–canonical Gospel of Peter that it was Roman custom to release one Jewish prisoner at the time of the Passover. Aside from these sources, however, there is no record of this custom. Think of it as a literary device to set up the Barabbas story. If they are going to blame the crucifixion of Jesus on the Jews, the Gospel writers need the throngs of Jews to call for the release of someone other than Jesus, and they solve their problem with the invention of Barabbas.

The notion that the Gospels are not always, well, gospel, may be difficult for some to accept. If you can't, don't. The rest of this book will still be of value to you. But before you dismiss my argument, hear me out. Stay with me long enough to discover whether the facts in the Gospels themselves suggest something highly improbable, if not, as I claim, downright impossible.

Pilate, the Roman governor, was such a tyrant that he was once called back to Rome and ordered to tone down his brutality. Imagine that: he was excessively brutal even by Roman standards! Is this the type of man who would release any prisoners, let alone like Barabbas, whom John calls a *lēstēs*, a "revolutionary"? Barabbas wasn't some minor criminal, but a member of the Zealots, the Jewish terrorist underground. Is Pilate going to free a terrorist?

It makes no sense that Pilate, the most notorious of Rome's tyrants, would care about executing an innocent Jew like Jesus. He has already slaughtered thousands of innocents, why care about one more? Furthermore, if he was inclined to free a prisoner— something for which we have no evidence outside the story of the trial itself—it makes no sense for him to release a man convicted of murdering Roman soldiers. Someone who would no doubt go right back to murdering more as soon as he got out of jail.

So, even if there were two men in prison, Jesus and Barabbas, freeing Barabbas makes no sense. But I also want to suggest something far more daring. What if there was only one man imprisoned at the time, and it was Barabbas, and Barabbas was Jesus?

In the Greek texts of the New Testament, Barabbas is spelled *bar-Abbas*, a name that comes from the Aramaic, *Bar-Abba* (Son of the Father). In an early Greek manuscript of Matthew 27:15–18, we are told that Barabbas' full name was Jesus Barabbas, or Jesus Son of the Father. What are the odds that Pilate has two men in jail, each called Jesus Son of the Father? Slim to none, I suggest.

The truth is that Pilate had only one Jesus Barabbas in prison, only one man called Jesus Son of the Father, and the Jews who demonstrated for the release of Jesus Barabbas on Good Friday were the same Jews who welcomed Jesus Son of the Father to Jerusalem with open arms on Palm Sunday. While it may be true that Caiaphas and his chief priests wished to see Jesus dead, the Jews themselves did not. When they call for the liberation of Barabbas they are calling for the liberation of Jesus, Son of the Father, the same Jesus Christians call the Christ.

Jesus was not an enemy of the Jews, although, like his fellow Pharisees, he may have been opposed by the Sadducees. On the contrary, Jesus, like his fellow

Pharisees, was a rabbi seeking to articulate his vision of Judaism and teach it to whoever would listen. And at the heart of this Judaism, this religion of Jesus, are the two touchstone passages of the Torah he cites in Mark and Matthew: Deuteronomy 6:4–9, and Leviticus 19:18. It is to these two texts that we now turn our attention, taking them a bit at time in the same way we examined the 23rd Psalm.

Because both Mark and Matthew deal with the same story, I will blend elements of both, and in this way allow us to get the most out of Jesus' teaching. I will also fill in some text from Deuteronomy that the Gospels do not cite because the Jews to whom Jesus spoke would have discussed it as they listened to him.

To be fair to both Mark and Matthew, let us examine both texts using my translation which keeps some of the original Hebrew words of Jesus missing in both the Greek and English versions:

Mark 12: 28–34

One of the scribes came near and ... asked him, "Which mitzvah is the first of all?" Jesus answered, "The first is, *Hear, O Israel: the Lord our God, the Lord is one; you shall love the*

Lord your God with all your heart, and with all your soul, and with all your mind, and with all your strength. The second is this, *You shall love your neighbor as yourself.* There are no mitzvot greater than these." Then the scribe said to him, "You are right, Rabbi ... this is much more important than all whole burnt offerings and sacrifices." When Jesus saw that he answered wisely, he said to him, "You are not far from the kingdom of God." After that no one dared to ask him any question.

Matthew 22:34–40

When the Pharisees heard that he had silenced the Sadducees, they gathered together, and one of them, a rabbi, asked him a question to test him. "Rabbi, which *mitzvah* in the Torah is the greatest?" He said to him, "*You shall love the Lord your God with all your heart, and with all your soul, and with all your mind.* This is the greatest and first mitzvah. And a second is like it: *You shall love your neighbor as yourself.* On these two mitzvot hang the entire Torah and Nevi'im (prophets)."

One of them, a rabbi

In Mark the questioner is a scribe, in some English translations of Matthew he is a lawyer. In fact both terms refer to rabbis. There were no lawyers in ancient Israel other than rabbis and scribes. The only law was the religious law and the only people charged with interpreting it were rabbis. And since all rabbis were Pharisees, some conservative (following Shammai) and some liberal (following Hillel), this fellow was a Pharisee as well.

asked him a question to test him

The idea of testing is not meant to suggest hostility toward Jesus. On the contrary, it is the ultimate sign of respect among rabbis. Argument and debate are at the heart of Pharisaic pedagogy; it is how rabbis learn from and teach one another. It is common for rabbis to challenge one another, and there is no expectation that all rabbis will agree with one another. Indeed, disagreement is thought to be intrinsic to the rabbinic method.

The educational motto of the rabbis is *Elu v'Elu Divrei Elohim Chayyim*, "These words and those words are both the words of the Living God," as long as the opinions are part of an honest and sincere effort to determine the meaning of the Torah and the right way one is to live. All opinions, even those that directly contradict one another, are said to be the Words of the Living God, legitimate interpretations of the Torah if offered with the proper intent.

Rabbi, which of the Torah's mitzvot is the greatest?

The unnamed rabbi who questions Jesus refers to Jesus as a rabbi. This is no small thing. Too often we imagine that rabbi simply means "teacher," and suggests nothing more. This is incorrect. Rabbi actually means "my master" and is a term used only in reference to those whose scholarship merits their being called a master of the Torah. If this unnamed rabbi intended to disrespect Jesus he would not have called him rabbi.

I have chosen to use the Hebrew words *mitzvah* and *mitzvot* (plural of *mitzvah*) rather than "command" and "commandments" because these are the terms Jesus would have used. Using the Hebrew allows us to uncover a deeper meaning than the standard English translation allows.

Mitzvot are the means by which Jews encounter God and live godly lives. What is being asked of Jesus is this: "Rabbi, tell me how best to meet God, and make my life a vehicle for godliness?"

Jesus answers by citing two passages of the Torah, one from Deuteronomy, the other from Leviticus. Mark gives us the fuller version: "Hear, O Israel: the Lord your God, the Lord is one; you shall love the Lord your God with all your heart, and with all your soul, and with all your mind, and with all your strength" (Deuteronomy 6:4–5, Mark 12:29–30), and Matthew gives us the shorter: "You shall love the Lord your God with all your heart, and with all your soul, and with all your mind" (Deuteronomy 6:5, Matthew 22:37). The second is Leviticus 19:18: "You shall love your neighbor as yourself."

The first text cited by Jesus is considered two connected texts in Judaism. The first is called the *Shema* (Listen) and the second is called the *Ve'ahavta* (You Shall Love). They are said together as part of our daily liturgy, and have been since long before Jesus' day. Thus, when he cited these texts he didn't have to recite the entire text but only enough to make his meaning clear. This is why Matthew abbreviated Jesus' words even more, knowing that the Jews who would read his Gospel would know to add the additional material.

Today, however, it is Christians rather than Jews who hear the Gospels of Mark and Matthew, and they may not—and most likely do not—make the larger association that Jesus and his listeners would have made. To help with this we need to explore the complete *Shema* and *Ve'ahavta*.

Listen

What do you do when you try to listen intently? First, you seek to shut out all ambient noise, both within you and around you. Then your body becomes very still, almost immobile. Every nerve ending is striving to work in concert with your ears to maximize your ability to hear. For a moment, listening is all there is. The very notion of a "you" that is listening is gone. There is just full-bodied listening.

You have certainly experienced this at some point in your life. Listening closely to the divine compositions of Mozart, perhaps, you found that for a time you were not aware that you were listening; there was hearing without a hearer. Or, attending to the words of a great orator or poet, you suddenly discovered that time had passed and knowledge had been gained without your ever being aware of either. Or, on a sadder note, when straining to hear a loved one sobbingly tell of a tragedy, or even upon hearing a strange noise in your home or in a parking lot when you are all alone, you have experienced the kind of intense listening Jesus and the Torah are talking about.

Israel

The Hebrew word *Yisrael* (Israel) is the name given to Jacob by the angel with whom he wrestled at Jabbok's ford (Genesis 32:22), and the name taken by all of his descendants to refer to the Hebrew people. *Yisrael* means "one who wrestles" (*yisra*) "*with God*" (*El*). You wrestle with God when you wrestle with yourself in pursuit of godliness.

The rabbis of Jesus' time and ours teach that humans are born innocent, not good or evil. We are neither saints nor sinners, but *bennoni*—people with a capacity for good and a capacity for evil. Our whole lives are a wrestling match between these competing desires,

91

and there is never a winner. Jacob does not defeat his opponent, nor is he defeated by him. Good does not triumph over evil, nor evil over good. Neither of our two competing desires, our *Yetzer haTov* (capacity for good) and our *Yetzer haRah* (capacity for evil), defeats the other. Rather, the second becomes the servant of the first.

The Yetzer haRah is that aspect of ourselves that focuses on self, and which, if not checked by the Yetzer haTov, can lead to selfishness. The Yetzer haTov is that aspect of ourselves that focuses on selflessness, which, if not checked by the Yetzer haRah, can lead to self hatred. The rabbis teach us to balance these two, to be both for ourselves and for others at the same time. As Jesus' own rabbi, Hillel, put it: "If I am not for myself, who will be for me? But, if I am only for myself, what am I? And if not now, when?" (Pirke Avot 1:14)

Like Jacob, when we achieve this balance of concern for both self and other we become Yisrael, Godwrestlers seeking to bring out the deepest meaning of life by seeing to the wellbeing of all the living. We see this in the closing verses of the story of Jacob and his brother Esau.

Immediately after Jacob receives the name Yisrael,

he looks up and sees his brother approaching at the head of an army of 400 warriors (Genesis 33:1). Jacob fully expects to die at his brother's hand, but something has changed—namely, Jacob himself. Rather than flee from his brother as he did decades earlier, he races to meet him, bowing down seven times as an act of surrender and humility. Taken aback, Esau runs ahead of his soldiers and the two brothers embrace and cry. The first act of Israel is to tearfully reconcile with your enemy (Genesis 33:4). You know you are Israel when you, as Jesus put it, love your enemy and pray for those who persecute you (Matthew 5:44).

Esau then invites his brother to travel with him, but Jacob/Israel declines explaining that while Esau travels at the pace of a warrior, Jacob/Israel now travels slowly at the pace of the children and the nursing calves and babies for whom he is responsible (Genesis 33:14). In other words, Jacob who used to be concerned with his own power and status, is now Israel, the servant of what Jesus will come to call "the least of these" (Matthew 25:40).

93

When the Torah and Jesus ask us to listen, they ask us to listen to the needs of the powerless, as did Israel, and to fulfill them.

YHVH is our God

YHVH is the unpronounceable Hebrew Name of God. We have dealt with this Name in our earlier discussion of the 23rd Psalm. It is unfortunate that the ancient rabbis chose the Hebrew word *Adonai* as their stand in for the Unpronounceable Name. *Adonai* means "Lord," which is why our English Bibles speak of God as Lord when the Hebrew Bible does not.

Adonai/Lord carries with it a masculine connotation that YHVH does not, and implies a static hierarchy that is anathema to the Hebrew original. YHVH, as you might remember, isn't even a noun. It's a verb, a form of the Hebrew verb "to be." God isn't a being, not even the Supreme Being, but *be–ing* itself. God is what is.

The best understanding we have of YHVH in the Torah comes from Moses' encounter with God at the Burning Bush (Exodus 3:1-21). It is there that God reveals the essence of divinity as *Ehyeh asher Ehyeh*: not just the static "I am what I am" of so many Bibles, but the dynamic "I will be whatever I will be" (Exodus 3:14). God is both the eternal and unchanging "I am" and the temporal and changing "I shall be." God is all that is. As a wave arising in and returning to the ocean, so everything arises in and returns to God. You are God, just not all of God.

This is what Jesus points to when he says, "I am the vine and you are the branches. Those who remain in me, and I in them, will yield much fruit" (John 15:5), and what the Apostle Paul means when he says, "For in God we live and move and have our being" (Acts 17:28). The extent to which this is true for you is the extent to which you are open to a profound sense of inner peace and tranquility. The extent to which you are ignorant of this truth is the extent to which you are haunted by fear and plagued by unnecessary suffering.

YHVH is One

Just as there is no separation between an ocean and its waves, there is no separation between God and creation. It is all God; it is all One. Rabbi Schneur Zalman of Liady, the 18th century founder of a mystical school of Judaism called CHaBaD, an acronym for Wisdom, Understanding, and Knowledge, asked why it is that Jews, even in Jesus' day, would repeat the *Sh'ma* several times a day if all it is saying is that

God is one and not, for example, seven. His answer is that we repeat the *Sh'ma* not to remember that there is only one God, but to remind ourselves that in the face of all perceptions to the contrary, everything that is, is one in, with, and as God. Oneness is not a numerical fact but an ontological reality. In the Jewish liturgy we read: "Know this day in the depths of your heart that YHVH is God; in the skys above and on the earth below there is nothing else" (*Ayn od*).

Ayn od, there is nothing else but God. The application of this fact to our daily lives is called Ethical Monotheism. Ethical Monotheism understands that the fundamental unity of all life in God requires a universal moral code rooted in divine reality. One God necessitates one world, one humanity, and one moral code—justice and compassion for all. These two words, *YHVH Echad*/God is One, are the heart of the religion of Jesus. All reality is YHVH, the One Ineffable Unnameable Source and Substance of all being and becoming.

You Shall Love

This is a strange sentence: You *shall* love! Can love be commanded? No. No emotion can be "on tap," and any forced feelings of love are deceptive and misleading. Neither the Torah nor Jesus is commanding us to love. Rather, they are pointing out that if you listen so deeply that you experience the oneness of God in, with, and as all things, then you will be filled with love for God and all things.

"You shall love" is not a command, but the second half of a spiritual axiom: Do A, and B will surely follow; Listen and Love will surely follow.

Both the Torah and Jesus link listening and love, and this should be a surprise to no one because you hear the same thing from the people you love. Your friends, your children, your spouse or partner, what do they want from you the most? That you listen to them. Listening says we care; listening says they are important to us; listening says we will make the time and the effort to be present to another's pain and joy. Listening says *I love you*.

It is the very act of listening that engenders love. Listen and hear the absolute unity of all life in, with,

97

and as God, and you will be filled with love and compassion for all beings. There are no strangers in God; there is no other in God. *Ayn od*: there is no thing else but God.

With a Whole Heart

You cannot listen half-heartedly and you cannot love half-heartedly. Without wholeness, there is no love. The wholeness we are talking about is the awareness that Self and Other are both linked in the greater unity of God. If the love you feel doesn't reveal and reflect the unity of God with creation, and the unity of creation within God, it is not yet of the deep listening the Torah and Jesus are aiming for. We will explore this more fully when we come to Jesus' second great mitzvah.

With your every breath

Standard English translations render the Hebrew word *nefesh* as "soul" and *nafsh'cha*, the Hebrew word Jesus would have quoted in response to the rabbi's question, as "your soul." The problem with this translation is that the word "soul" implies a theology that the Torah lacks. A better and more literal translation would be "your breath."

Love God with every breath. There are two meanings here, reflecting two ways of using the breath: for speech and for silence. Breath is essential for speech. We cannot form words without filling consonants with the breath of vowels. So, how do we love God with our speech? By using our words to heal rather than to harm. Life and death are in the power of the tongue (Proverbs 18:21). Loving God with every breath is speaking loving words with every breath.

Breath is also essential to silence, the deep silence that allows us to listen to the unity of God. Every meditative system uses the breath as a tool for inner stillness and deep spiritual awakening. "And YHVH formed the earthling from the dust of the earth, and blew into the earthling the Breath of Life, and it was then that the earthling became a living being" (Genesis 2:7). God's out-breath is our in-breath. Every time we inhale, we breathe in the Breath of Life; every time we exhale, we return that gift to God. The rhythm of this breathing leads us to the still mind that listens in such a loving way as to transform us into Yisrael.

With all you have and are

The Hebrew here is *me'odecha*, which most English Bibles translate as "strength," but which is better understood as "all that we have and are." Literally, *me'odecha* means "your very-ness," suggesting that you are to love God as your very essence, everything that makes you who you are.

Spiritual awakening is not separate from every-day living, and spiritual practice must engage every-day actions. We love God with all we have and are by making certain that our dealings with each other and with nature are in accord with the highest ethical and moral standards we can muster. This means bringing our consumption in line with our highest ethical and environmental standards. It means using our wealth to help the poor. It means realizing that we were cre-ated to tend the Garden (Genesis 2:15), not to turn it into our own private playground.

There is much confusion over the story of creation in the Book of Genesis. For centuries, the Western world has taken the mitzvah to "subdue the earth" (Genesis 1:28) as license to exploit nature for our own narrow ends. If we drive species to extinction as we

100

populate the earth, so be it; if we deplete her natural resources and weaken her resiliency as we subdue the earth, well, that is what God intended. But it is not what God intended:

> Now all the trees of the field were not yet on the earth and all the herb of the field had not yet sprouted because YHVH God had not sent rain upon the earth and there was no human to till the soil (Genesis 2:5). YHVH God took the human and placed him in the Garden of Eden to till and to preserve it (Genesis 2:15).

What was God's intention? To create a world where all creatures work together to bring out the richness inherent in the earth. What is the purpose of humanity? To till and preserve. We are necessary and responsible for both the productivity of the earth and her preservation. We are as necessary to life as rain is. We are part of the process by which the unfolding of life happens. We need to remind ourselves of these truths if we are to love God with all we have and are.

Before we leave this section we should note that Mark renders this passage as "all your mind and all your strength," and Matthew shortens it to "all your mind." It is hard to know if the Gospel writers are quoting Jesus accurately, or if they are quoting the Torah inaccurately. While you can translate *me'odecha* as "strength," there is no way to work the word "mind" into the text at all. But perhaps Jesus is deliberately adding "mind" to the Torah, and, if so, what might this mean?

Mind could refer to thoughts; we are to love God with all our thoughts. This would require an effort of will few of us could muster. After all, we only know if our thoughts are loving or not only after we have thought them. If this is so, Jesus is putting us in an untenable position quite at odds with the rest of the text he is quoting.

Let me offer an alternative. Mind refers to our sense of self. It is the mind that generates the story of "I, me, and mine," and Jesus could be challenging us to dedicate all three to the love of God. How? By adding "neighbor" to the mix. When we can see that being for myself necessitates being for my neighbor as well, then we have the wholeness the Torah and Jesus are asking us to cultivate. We love God when we love our neighbor as our self. We will speak more of this shortly. For the time being, let's move on to the rest of the passage as Jesus would have prayed it multiple times a day, as Jews continue to do today.

Keep these words

What words? These words: *sh'ma* and *ve'ahavta*, listen and love. Religion is prone to complexity; spirituality is simple. Theology is given to arcane discourse; God is everyday reality. Religion establishes hierarchies of power; spirit is everywhere and available to all. The Torah and Jesus are warning us: Do not get distracted by the sophistry of religion; focus on what is essential —listening and loving.

That I am commanding you this day

This day. Today. Now. Don't imagine that listening and loving are things of the past, or ideals to be realized in the future. They are commandments, mitzvot, our means of meeting God and living godliness in this and every moment.

103

Upon your heart

These words of God are laid upon your heart, they are already an intimate part of your very being. You lack nothing (just as we learned in Psalm 23); you need do nothing other than reclaim that which is intrinsically yours: the innate capacity to listen and love.

It is natural to imagine that truth is hard to find and thereby excuse ourselves from finding it. But the Torah tells us that truth is not hidden or distant at all:

> It is not in heaven that you should excuse yourselves by saying, "Who can ascend to heaven for us and take it for us so that we can listen and do what is right?" It is not across the sea that you should excuse yourselves saying, "Who can cross the ocean for us and take it for us that we can listen and do what is right?" Rather it is very near to you, it is in your mouth and in your heart to perform it. (Deuteronomy 30:11)

You already know what is true. You were born knowing. You may pretend to you have never known for the simple fact that if you admit to knowing, you are obligated to doing, and the doing can be tough. Living an authentic spiritual life obligates us to continuous listening and loving, not once and forever. It is listening and loving in this moment and this moment and this moment again.

Teach them to your children

It is not enough for you to listen and love, you must teach your children to do so as well. And if you happen not to have children, then teach other people's children. Each generation is obligated to teach the next.

How do you teach this? By living it yourself. Mentoring and modeling the act of listening and loving is a challenge each us of must address in our own way. What follows will assist you in your mentoring and modeling.

Speak of them while sitting in your house

Talk with those closest to you about the practice of listening and loving. We are accustomed to televised public service announcements on television urging us to talk to our children about sex, drugs, drinking, and smoking. The Torah and Jesus are asking us to do the same in relation to God and godliness.

In some communities we ask children to consider *What would Jesus do?* In others, *What would Buddha do?* In my own community, I urge people to teach their children to ask *What would a mensch do?*

A mensch is a person who listens and loves. A mensch is a person who recognizes her capacity for both good and evil and works deliberately to assure that the former dictates her actions rather than the latter. Asking *What would a mensch do?* is an easy way to engage children (and adults) in a serious examination of personal ethics and morality.

Walking on your path

The Torah isn't referring to some ethereal notion of a spiritual path, but to actual roads and streets. Your practice of listening and loving must include those who live with you in your home and everyone you meet outside of it. Spirituality has to be carried into the streets. It has to make a difference in the world.

When you lie down

Just before we fall asleep at night there are moments when the separate self fades. There is a lightness about us that is too subtle for words. At that time we should listen to the lessons of the day now ending, asking ourselves, who did we help today, and whom did we harm? To whom do we need to thank tomorrow, and to whom do we need to apologize? What changes are needed to assure that we are a little more holy for having learned from the experiences of today? Listen to the answers and take action tomorrow as an act of love.

And when you rise up

The four postures mentioned in the *Ve'ahavta* verses are sitting, walking, lying down, and rising up. They are often called the essential postures of humankind. Everything we do is a variation of these four movements. The *Ve'ahavta* is biblical yoga. Each of these postures is linked with awakening to God and godliness through listening and loving.

At the moment of initial wakefulness, we are not yet preoccupied with self; there is a stillness and

107

openness about us. This is a moment for simply listening; your mind and body are not yet stirred to distraction. If you wait and listen without strain, every once in while you will hear with your entire body/mind the oneness that is God. When such a hearing comes to you, honor it completely. The experience may last only a second, and when it passes, you must make a careful transition to full wakefulness so as not to lose the memory in the distractions of the discursive mind.

After resting for a few more moments, say something like, "With a thankful and grateful heart, I honor the return of consciousness. May I live the day's unfolding with compassion and foster faith in the One Who is All."

Bind them as a sign upon your hand and between your eyes

The ancient rabbis saw in this phrase the mitzvah of *tefillin*, the black boxes containing the two texts we are examining that are worn on the head and arm during morning prayers. The intent of tefillin is to unite mind, heart, and hand in service to God and godliness. While you may choose to experiment with actual tefillin, I suspect you will benefit most from contemplating the attributes of godliness represented by the wearing of tefillin: Presence, Compassion, Tenderness, Patience, Forbearance, Kindness, Awareness, Love, Forgiveness, and Freedom. These are the attributes of love that arise when you listen with a whole heart.

Fix them upon the doorposts of your house

It is from this text that the rabbis derived the mitzvah of *mezuzah*. The word mezuzah literally means "doorpost," but it has now come to refer to the decorative cases containing the *Sh'ma* and *Ve'ahavta* that Jews place on the doorposts of their homes, inside and out. *Mezuzot* (the plural of mezuzah) are reminders calling you to listen and love.

While you may choose to purchase actual mezuzot, you may also substitute some other reminder. Place the mezuzah about one-third of the way down the righthand doorpost when facing the doorway as if to enter the room. Some people angle the mezuzah about 45 degrees so that the top of the casing is slanted toward the room. Others prefer to keep the mezuzah upright. As you attach each mezuzah, recite the following: "Blessed is the Source of Life Who offers me this reminder to listen and love."

As you enter a room with a mezuzah on the doorpost, take a moment to let the reminder sink in, so that every one of your encounters in the room is defined by deep listening and the love that such listening releases.

And upon your gates

When I come home at the end of a tiring day, the mezuzah by my front door says to me, "Don't let the tumult of the day disturb the peace of your home." When I leave home in the morning, the mezuzah says to me, "Take a bit of this peace with you into the world." Both messages are wise and welcome, but both remain within the context of my household. When we set mezuzot on our gates, we are doing something different.

Here the mezuzah reminds us that the world, too, is our home and all earth's creatures are part of our household. Placing mezuzot upon our gates challenges us to mark every meeting, every coming in and every going out, with listening and love.

If you have no gate, think about these things metaphorically. Gates are the place of meeting between self and other. They signify where the boundary of self is open to the presence of the other. Right there at that place of profound meeting we recognize the other as a manifestation of God just as we ourselves are manifestations of God.

Having taken this excursion into the full text of the *Sh'ma* and *Ve'ahavta* to which Jesus alluded, let's return to the Second Great Commandment: Love your neighbor as yourself.

You shall love your neighbor as yourself

Whenever this text comes up in my university class on the Bible, I can count on students to misread it in this way, "You shall love your neighbor as you love yourself." We all too often assume that self love is a prerequisite for loving others. But this is not what the Torah or Jesus teach. You are to love your neighbor regardless of how you feel about yourself. In fact, loving your neighbor isn't about feelings at all.

Loving your neighbor means treating her according to what we have come to call the Golden Rule. The story about the Gentile and Hillel contains the earlier version of the Golden Rule that Jesus would have learned from his teachers: "That which is hateful to you, do not do to another. This is the whole of Torah. All the rest is commentary. Now, go and study it."

Hillel's negative expression of the Golden Rule is balanced by Jesus' positive formulation in Matthew 7:12, "In everything do to others as you would have them do to you; for this is the Torah and the Prophets." Regardless of which version you prefer, they both speak to the same goal: loving one's neighbor as oneself.

Love here means mutual respect. Just as I would not want to be exploited, lied to, cheated, or abused, so I must not exploit, lie to, cheat, or abuse another. Because we are talking about respect and mutuality rather than any emotional or romantic sense of love, we can understand why Jesus might challenge us to love our enemies as well.

Just as David believed that God will provide a table of reconciliation at which we and our enemies, like

Jacob and Esau, might meet and make peace, so Hillel and Jesus believed that God provides us with the capacity to treat with respect even those who oppose us. But there is more to this teaching.

When we misread the text so that it speaks of self love, we fail to glean the deeper meaning of "as yourself."

Your neighbor is a part of yourself. Remember that all beings are one in God, the Source and Substance of all creation. Your neighbor, the "other," is a part of you in the same way as *up* is a part of *down,* as *in* is a part of *out*, and as *front* is a part of *back*. In the same way, *self* is a part of *other* and *neighbor* is a part of *yourself.*

There is a Jewish teaching that applies here:

If I am I, and you are you, then
I am merely I, and you are merely you. But
If I am I because you are you, then
I am not merely I, and you are not merely you.

You are not merely you. You do not exist in isolation. You do not create the world you encounter, you respond to it. And in that response you determine who you are. At the heart of that encounter is the other, the neighbor, the stranger, the friend, the enemy—human

113

and otherwise. Your encounter with the other defines you. How should you meet the other? By listening and loving. And when you do listen and you do love, you discover that the other is part of you; your neighbor is yourself, and you love them both.

Rabbi Nachman of Breslov, the 18th century mystic and sage, discovered something else in this text. The Hebrew original is, like the Hebrew Bible as a whole, without vowels. The reader of the text supplies the vowels and usually does so in standardized ways. The Hebrew that we translate as "Love your neighbor as yourself," is pronounced *Ve'ahavta et rayecha k'mocha.* Rabbi Nachman noticed that the same sentence could legitimately, if unconventionally, be vocalized this way: *Ve'ahavta et rahecha k'mocha.* The difference between *rey-echa* and *rah-echa* is huge. *Rey-echa* means "your neighbor," *rah-echa* means "your evil." The Torah may be challenging you to love not only your neighbor but your own dark side, your own Yetzer haRah (capacity for evil) as part of yourself.

The connection is as follows: rather than accept and learn to love (in effect, bind to our capacity for good) the shadow side of ourselves, we often deny we have a shadow side and unconsciously project it onto our neighbor or "the other." What we dislike and fear about ourselves we project onto them. The Torah may be telling us to reclaim our shadow, to withdraw the projection, to love even our capacity for evil (though not to indulge it), and to free the neighbor from carrying our shadow. At which time we might meet them as they are and not as we imagine them to be.

You are right, rabbi

The unnamed questioner of Jesus in Mark recognizes the rightness of Jesus' teaching, saying, "This is much more important than all whole burnt offerings and sacrifices." Most likely he sees it as a restatement of Hillel's claim that the Golden Rule is the "whole of the Torah," the link which Matthew makes plain in his version of the story wherein Jesus himself paraphrases Hillel saying, "On these two mitzvot hang the entire Torah and Prophets."

The difference between Mark and Matthew on this point is that in Mark's version, Jesus' teaching replaces the sacrifices in the Temple, while for Matthew (and Hillel) they replace all the other teachings of the Torah and the Prophets. Together, Mark and Matthew

115

have reinvented the entirety of Judaism as both the Sadducees and the Pharisees understand it, replacing the rituals of the Temple and the traditions of the rabbis with love—love of God and love of neighbor.

The difference between Jesus and Hillel on this point is subtle, but worth mentioning. While both Hillel and Jesus place love at the heart of their Judaisms, Hillel sees a role for the rest of the tradition where Jesus does not. For Hillel, the rest of Judaism is commentary; that is, the entirety of the Jewish law and custom should be interpreted in light of the Golden Rule and seen as a means for living it in everyday life. For Jesus, no commentary is necessary. Listening and loving are sufficient in and of themselves.

When Jesus saw that he answered wisely

What does it mean that Jesus saw that the man answered wisely? Did the man do more than simply affirm the rightness of Jesus' teaching? Yes, he did do more: He saw it as the new Judaism beyond priests, priest craft, and Temple sacrifices. He not only agreed that to listen and to love—to love God and to love the other—is at the center of Judaism, at that instant he realized listening and loving *was* Judaism. We know this because in Mark's Gospel it is the man and not Jesus who proclaims love as a replacement for the Judaism of the Temple. Seeing this, Jesus knew him to be wise.

You are not far from the kingdom of God

Given the man's wisdom, why is he not yet in the kingdom of God? Why is he only "not far" away from it? What is missing?

The Kingdom of God is not an idea to be debated, but an action to be lived. What the man had yet to do, and what he may not have had the courage to do, is live the love the Torah, Hillel, and Jesus demand. Unless and until we "walk at the pace of the nursing calves and babies," unless and until we "do unto the least of these," we are not yet in the Kingdom of God.

To listen and to love isn't a philosophy but a program for living. And until we make it a way of life— our way of life—the Kingdom is not yet manifest.

117

After that no one dared to ask him any question.

This line only appears in Mark's Gospel. Understanding the meaning of this final line depends upon whether you believe the questioner is trying to attack Jesus with his question or to honor him by asking it. If you think the former is true, then it is Jesus' cleverness that silences the people and ends the questioning. He is too wise to be trapped with these tests, so there is no point in testing him further.

I don't think the man was attacking Jesus, but honoring him (as one would any other rabbi) by asking him to articulate the heart of his teaching. This unnamed man did for Jesus what the unnamed Gentile did for Hillel: allow each sage to utter his deepest truth in a single teaching.

With this understanding in mind, the reason none dared ask another question is that none dared deny the truth of what Jesus had said. If listening is the way to love, love is the way to godliness; and if godliness is defined as treating others as you would be treated, what other questions are there? Anything more would muddy the waters.

118

I love this final line of Mark. It speaks to me of the profound silence that arises when a great insight is grasped. There is nothing more to say. There is no need to speak. The silence confirms the truth of what was said and what was heard. And with that in mind, let me be silent as well.

ABOUT THE
AUTHOR

BORN YIRACHMIEL BEN YISROEL V'SARAH in 1951, Rami spent several years in kindergarten trying to learn to pronounce his name. Being the only first grader who had to shave, Rami was promoted through school quickly, earning both rabbinic ordination and a Ph.D. Forced to get a job at age thirty, Rami led a congregation for twenty years where he learned that irony, humor, and iconoclasm made for poor bedside manner, and honesty was rarely the best policy when it came to religion. Author of over two dozen books and hundreds of essays, Rami writes a regular column for *Spirituality & Health* magazine entitled "Roadside Assistance for the Spiritual Traveler."